M000218137

EDUCATION OR IMITATION?

Bible Interpretation for Dummies
Like You and Me

Curtis Allen

Shout outs:
To my wife, Betsy, and our sons Santiago, Giovanni,
and Mateo. And to my church family at The Rock!
May we all know our Bibles well enough
to imitate Jesus.
- Curtis Allen

CruciformPress

CruciformPress.com | info@CruciformPress.com

"Curt Allen's book on interpreting the Bible is wonderfully practical and clear, giving believers basic principles for understanding God's Word. He rightly emphasizes that every believer can understand the Bible. It isn't necessary to be a scholar or preacher or to know Greek and Hebrew to grasp the Scriptures. Certainly, we are helped by teachers and scholars, but we can understand the Bible ourselves and need to test whatever others say by the Scriptures. Allen also shows that the Bible is Christ-centered. We are only reading the Bible rightly if we are seeing Jesus Christ, our crucified and risen Lord, in its pages. At the same time, the Bible is not just meant to be understood but to be lived out in our everyday lives. I recommend gladly such an accessible, Christ-centered, and practical book on interpreting the Scriptures."

Thomas R. Schreiner, James Buchanan Harrison Professor of New Testament Interpretation, Southern Baptist Theological Seminary

"Gritty. Real. Straight. That's what you'll find in Curt Allen's treatment of Bible interpretation, *Education or Imitation?* And that's what we need because airy, heady, abstract works on Bible interpretation fail to do the one thing they're written for – teach and inspire us to read, interpret and apply the Bible. If you want it straight, read this book."

Thabiti Anyabwile, Author; Senior Pastor, First Baptist Church, Grand Cayman; Council Member, The Gospel Coalition

Table of Contents

Chapters

Education or Imitation? — Bible Interpretation for Dummies Like You and Me

Print ISBN: 978-1-936760-41-1
ePub ISBN: 978-1-936760-43-5
Mobipocket ISBN: 978-1-936760-42-8

One
WHY INTERPRETATION MATTERS IN EVERYTHING

What You Don't Know Can Kill You

I sat in a smoke-filled room in an apartment complex in Laurel, Maryland, watching Jerry and José. They were city boys from New York, and they had the undivided attention of some dudes from my 'hood.

The rest of us in the room called ourselves The Second Gen, or The Gen. We were the newest generation of street thugs active in and around Washington, DC. All of us were criminals by nature and most of us were criminals under the law. Drugs, guns, drug deals, violent crime, handcuffs, mug shots, indictments, court cases, and prison time were just part of our lifestyle. At that time, DC was known as the murder capital of the United States, and for good reason.

Even though I was one of the best-known drug

dealers in the area, I was one of the few from The Gen
who hadn't been arrested yet. I made thousands of dollars
a week selling crack cocaine to people from all over the
place. I was proud of it, and I was proud of the fact that
my 'hood respected me for it. I respected them, too. I had
learned a lot about the street game from these dudes. They
had taught me how to survive on evil streets.

A nother thing I respected about these guys was
their ability to read people. I had always been good at
this myself and, as we say in the street, "game recognizes
game." You respect others who are like you. I trusted
these dudes with my life. We did a lot together. We sold
and used drugs, shot guns at rival gangs, went on trips to
New York and Atlantic City just to blow money and find
girls, recorded many rap songs, and often lived in each
other's apartments. We were family.

We respected and trusted no one more than each
other, which is why I was a little surprised to see the kind
of respect Jerry and José were getting. We hardly knew
these guys. My man "D" had met them and brought them
to our apartment. I didn't like that because we sold crack
out of that apartment and smoked a lot of weed there. Not
to mention that undercover police were always on the
prowl posing as fellow drug dealers and users. They had
locked up many of our friends, and for that reason alone
we always played it extra cautious around people we
didn't really know.

Nonetheless, in walks D with Jerry and José. I
quickly began hiding guns, drugs, and other things as
they all came in the front door. On the kitchen counter in

plain sight was enough illegal paraphernalia to warrant a federal drug raid. I was irritated at D for being so stupid as to bring two dudes we didn't know to the apartment and not call us ahead of time to make sure we weren't "dirty." If we were, and Jerry and José had been undercover, my "not arrested yet" streak would be over.

I hid what I could in the back room and came out to meet Jerry and José. I thought it would be a quick hello/goodbye type of thing, but as time went on, it became clear they weren't going anywhere. The room was filled with weed smoke as we heard story after story about the Bronx. Jerry and José were real comical dudes, with accents funnier than the stories they were telling. José's Puerto Rican twist on DC slang kept me laughing even when he wasn't trying to be funny.

After a while they began talking about things that were more serious. Jerry, who seemed to be the leader, started saying he could get us kilos of cocaine for a price that seemed too good to be true. At that time, most of us would buy crack, smokeable cocaine. But everybody wanted to get their hands on straight cocaine because you could cut it – add other things to it – and either make it more powerful to the user, more desirable on the street because it was something special, or simply more profitable to you as the dealer. I knew that if I got my hands on a kilo, I would cut it with another drug to make it the best product on the streets. Once you get a reputation for having that "bomb" product, you could sell water to a whale.

As Jerry was talking I kept glancing at other guys. I was trying to read how *they* were reading *him*, and it seemed to me like Jerry had my friends in the palm of his hand. I had been suspicious at first, but I was letting up on that since all these guys I respected for their street discernment were embracing Jerry and José. Just as I was about to give these dudes the green light of approval in my own mind, I noticed Jerry and José look at each other. It wasn't an obvious glance, but it caught my attention. The look seemed to communicate something that wasn't good. At least, not good for my friends and me. I looked around again at other guys to see if they had noticed. Everyone seemed to carry on as if it was business as usual. I didn't. I played it like I was all-in, but my radar was up, and it was pointed directly at Jerry and José.

As time went by the conversation seemed to fade into unintelligible mumbling. The more weed I smoked, the more tired I got. Eventually, I passed out. The next morning I woke up with a sharp pain in my side after sleeping in an unnatural position.

Jerry, José, and D were gone. I was groggy, both from a weed hangover and a lack of decent sleep. I scanned the room to see if anything looked odd, but it all seemed normal. I went to the back room to check if the stuff I hid the night before was still there. It was. I was relieved. Then I remembered the look that Jerry and José gave each other. I started to wonder if I was just overreacting.

I wasn't.

For most of the next several days I was out of the apartment, so I didn't see Jerry and José myself, but I knew they had been around. A week came and went. Then one day I was there with some of the other dudes when Jerry and José came to the door. This time, D wasn't with them. I remember thinking, *Wow, it only takes a week before these guys are coming here by themselves.* I knew they had an apartment in the same complex, so it seemed pretty clear we were going to be seeing them a lot.

We were all sitting in the living room. I decided not to get high because Jerry and José were still triggering my Spidey sense. With my head clear, it just became more and more obvious to me that there was something off about these guys. I knew they weren't undercover, but I figured they were "hot" – the kind of people in the thug world who tend to draw unwanted attention to themselves, like from the police. I was a criminal, and so far a highly successful one. The last thing I wanted was to have people around who were hot.

Afternoon drifted into evening and Jerry asked us if we wanted to go to a club with him. I hated clubs because I thought they were a waste of time and money. Not to mention all the mind games you have to play to get a girl's phone number and convince her to come back to your place. You can't really talk to a girl with music blasting, anyway. If I needed a second reason not to go, it was because I was pretty sure Jerry and José were trouble. A couple of my friends said that they were going, and I thought they were stupid. Didn't they see the fakeness in Jerry and José's body language? Those dudes were hot. Running around with them could get us all locked up, or worse.

Jerry and José left, promising to come back at 8:30. As soon as that apartment door closed, I told my friends I thought they were stupid to go with these guys. For 45 minutes we argued about what we thought of them and whether we really trusted them enough to let them hang out with The Gen. We were split. As 8 p.m. rolled around, I left to run errands. When I came back an hour or so later, I was glad to see that nobody had gone with Jerry and José.

By the next morning, we were all glad.

Saturday morning. The TV on in the apartment as usual. A news flash. Live coverage. We recognize the highway, the one right next to our apartment complex. All eyes are on the TV.

A call had come came in to the Maryland State Police about a suspicious-looking roll of rug on the shoulder of the road. When an officer responded to the call he noticed black hair sticking out of one end. Rolled up in the rug were three women, ages 19-25. They had been shot dead, wrapped in the rug, and dumped on the shoulder.

I had seen a lot of crazy things up to that point. I had been in shootouts, robberies, drug deals gone bad, and things I am too ashamed to mention. I thought nothing could really affect me anymore. I was wrong. We all were. Collectively, The Gen had seen enough wickedness that we were all too hard to let our emotions show. But we definitely shared in the horror of that moment as we watched the news. No one said anything for 10 minutes. I broke the silence.

"I don't know, yung. I hope them bamas didn't kill them three girls," I said, shaking my head, already believing they had. Silence answered me back, but I couldn't tell if the other dudes agreed with me. Maybe they were just in shock at how this had happened so nearby. That's when I realized that at any moment the police were going to be all over our neighborhood, and it was not going to be routine.

We would have to shut down. The whole area was now way too hot for us to keep selling crack out of the apartment. I decided I needed to distance myself from everyone for a bit. I followed my instincts and left the apartment. A couple of days later I learned that Jerry and José had done it. They had killed those girls. Jerry told D everything that happened, and D told us.

They had gone to the club that night, met the three girls, and brought them back to their apartment, four buildings away from ours. After getting high and drinking, Jerry asked one of the girls for sex. She said no. He tried repeatedly to convince her and each time she was more forceful with her answer. Before long, all the girls demanded to be taken to their cars back at the club. Jerry and José felt disrespected. They put the girls in their van, drove away, pulled off on a dark road, and shot them. Then they wrapped the three dead girls in a rug and dumped them off on the side of highway.

The whole time I was listening to this story, I kept going back to that look that I saw them give each other in our apartment. I knew there was something about them I didn't like. I knew these dudes were trouble. I just didn't know what kind.

A month after the murders, the police were closing in on Jerry and José. Jerry was afraid of getting ratted out, so he killed José. Three months later, the police caught Jerry and charged him with the murder of all three girls.

Jerry was sent to a prison where the brother of one of the girls was housed. This guy was a "gangsta," and that only meant one thing: the minute Jerry walked in that prison, he was as good as dead.

Bad Interpretation Can Kill You

Today, I still wonder what would have happened if I had gone to the club with Jerry and José. I may have had enough sense not to participate in all that took place that night, but it wouldn't have mattered much. I still would have been an accessory to three murders just by being with those guys. My life would be completely different; it might easily be over.

Every time I think about it, I am led back to that look that I noticed Jerry give to José. And then back to how I *interpreted* that look. I noticed something in their body language that made me distrust them, and today I attribute that perception entirely to the sovereign mercy of God.

If I had missed that look, or read it wrong, I might have missed all the other things that led me to be so cautious. I know that my interpretation of who Jerry and José were saved my life and probably some of my friend's lives. My interpretation led to application – I behaved differently because of my perceptions about what was true and what was false. This is the way it always goes. What you see, think, or feel informs what you do. If you interpret that walking down a certain street may be dangerous, then your application will probably be, *I'm not walking down that street!* Interpretation is a way of life for everyone every day.

There are many forms of interpretation. We explain, expound, judge, understand, and decipher everything around us to try to make sense of the world. We interpret a baby's cry to see if it is time to feed or time to nap. We interpret body language to see if the person we are on a date with likes us. We interpret tones of voice to know if someone is angry or not. We interpret emails and text messages based upon the person, the medium of communication, and the content. Exclamation points can be a sign of excitement or a sign of anger – depends how you interpret them.

We can't function without interpretation. We all interpret, and we all make decisions to act based on our interpretations. Those actions represent our application.

Life, in some ways, really is this simple. We are creatures who interpret everything and then act in a way that represents a response to that interpretation. This is often why we hate being confused. When you are confused, you cannot interpret events clearly, so you don't know what to do. Should you run or stay? Should you laugh or cry? Should you say yes or no? These are all questions of interpretation and application.

Interpretation and application are always linked – but they are not always *perfectly* linked. Having an accurate interpretation gives you the best start to making right application, and the better your interpretation, the more likely you are to move into proper application. What is the proverbial 20/20 hindsight, really? It's a reinterpretation of an event based on new knowledge – knowledge that could have changed our application for the better if we had had the benefit of it at first.

But it's possible – and sometimes it's easy – to have a solid interpretation and then choose the wrong application. This is the battle that we face continually as believers living in a fallen world. Based on our inheritance from Adam and Eve, we have within us a sinful nature that pulls us away from the process of right-interpretation-followed-by-right-application. Even when we rightly interpret God and his Word, sin rages within us to resist the application God requires. We often stop ourselves from recognizing truth and then applying it rightly.

This is an unseen war, and that's why we need a book to talk about it. In this book, I hope to provide a helpful and inspiring perspective on how we interpret and apply Scripture. It may be a perspective you haven't heard before.

Interpretation as Imitation

For many Christians the word "interpretation," as it applies to the Bible, can carry some negative baggage. *Isn't that what my pastor does before he preaches? Isn't that what commentators do before they can write their books?* Not many ever say it, but it's easy to start to think that interpretation is out of your league, reserved for the few who have ascended to the heights of clarity. The rest of us are down in dumb-boy land somewhere just trying to have a thirty-minute quiet time.

We would love to know what these people know, and we esteem them for their Bible knowledge. We are impressed with their rigorous pursuit of education and imagine we don't have the time or desire to do what they've done.

And that is exactly the problem. Bible interpretation has become too exclusive.

Who comes to your mind when you think of solid Bible interpreters? Do church fathers like Chrysostom and Augustine show up? Maybe Luther, Calvin, or Spurgeon? A few contemporary heavies like Piper, Sproul, Carson, and Keller definitely top the list. You might even go hard and say the Apostle Paul – good choice.

There's something to notice here. When we think "Bible interpreters," what comes up nearly every time? Brilliance and training. Without even being aware of it, we have come to see interpretation as being joined at the hip to serious education, big-time brainpower, and a particular gift of wisdom and insight. But I want to make the case that interpreting the Bible is not primarily about education or some unusual degree of gifting. And I want to do that mainly by pointing out what we can learn about Bible interpretation from the one obvious person missing from that list above of Bible interpretation heavies.

We forgot to mention Jesus.

The greatest interpreter of God's Word by a factor of infinity is Jesus the Christ – and he has called everyone who believes to *imitate him*.

As Christians, we realize we are supposed to imitate our Savior (Ephesians 5:1). But what does that look like? We know we can't imitate his death for sins. Our dying on a cross would only accomplish a lot of pain for us. Jesus was able to atone for sin because he never sinned, so we take that one off the list. Besides that obvious exception, you could say we are called to imitate Jesus in almost every way - it's just going to look different with us, not being members of the Trinity. Two quick examples.

<u>**Performing miracles.**</u> Jesus did a lot of extraordinary miracles. That is, he changed reality from one condition to another. Lazarus was changed from the condition of being dead to the condition of being alive. Water was changed to wine. A frightening storm became a great day for a boat ride.

Through us, sometimes in big ways and sometimes in small ways, God changes things in the world for the better all the time. Every now and then, something that a Christian does in and through Christ could probably be called a miracle, but most of the time it's just called life - a life in which God is actively involved. So that's one small way we imitate him.

<u>**Resisting Satan.**</u> Jesus went *mano a mano* with Satan in the wilderness, fighting to resist temptation. When you and I resist temptation, it usually falls a little short of an epic cosmic battle. I don't ever expect to meet the Devil personally, and I hope you don't either, but fighting against sin is another area in which we clearly are called to imitate Jesus.

The same is true with how Jesus relied on his Father, how he was devoted to prayer, how his behavior always glorified the Father, and how he did so many other things. We should try to imitate Jesus in all these areas. But on this big, complex question of imitation, let's sift things out in a slightly different way.

Jesus is the one mediator between God and man. Because of this, you might say that Jesus faces two ways at the same time. He faces toward God the Father, and he faces toward man. He faces toward God the Father *on behalf of* man, and he faces toward man *to draw us to* God the Father. During his earthly ministry, in all the things that Jesus did with his "man" face (the miracles and the consistent prayer life and the teachings and all the rest) he was really focused on just two things: evangelism and discipleship.

Jesus spent the majority of his three years in public ministry, as recorded in the Gospels, telling people to believe in him – *evangelizing* – and teaching new believers how to live – *discipling*. In fact, everything that Jesus did in his public ministry served one of these two basic goals – the same goals he left us with in the form of the Great Commission. That's why all believers, if we will imitate God, are called to evangelize and disciple, because when you come right down to it, this is what Jesus' life was about. So the life of the Christian should be the same.

Yet there is more.

Evangelism and discipleship are the beginning and the end of Jesus' ministry. What was in the middle? What I mean is: What were the means that produced the end? The answer may be simpler than you think.

Interpretation of the Word of God, spoken and applied, is the primary means that Jesus used. This is how he evangelized, and this is how he discipled. If we strip all the miracles and teachings of Jesus down to their essence, we find Jesus interpreting God's Word, and applying that teaching in real life. In the process, he gave us some clear insight into how all people, especially those who believe in him, are to interpret Scripture. He left us some breadcrumbs to follow. But for many, that path has been lost – for them, interpretation of Scripture has become more about education than imitation.

The typical Christian is satisfied leaving interpretation up to his pastor, or maybe a pastor in print. There's no question that commentaries can be great tools. I use them and love them, but when I read commentaries I sometimes think, *I could never have gotten what they got from these words.* These commentators are smart and can be intimidating.

We want to understand Scripture rightly, and commentaries can help us do that, but here's the issue. Is a degree from a good Bible college, or a postgraduate education from a solid seminary, the *only* path to rightly interpreting Scripture? Do you really think that's how God set it up? Are the rest of us left paralyzed until we read some smart guy's thoughts? I think not. At least not according to Jesus. A lot of what Jesus expects us to do is *imitate him in interpreting the Bible rightly.* And for any Christian, the call of imitation will walk hand in hand with interpretation.

Be imitators of God – be interpreters, like Jesus.

Although the task will not be easy, my hope is you will find that this short book gives you a good start. We need some help because, not only do we have to deal with our own insecurities about interpreting the Bible correctly; we are surrounded by a culture of bad interpretation.

Political pundits, weathermen, stock analysts, and my fantasy football team all regularly exemplify bad interpretation of available information. It is a sign of the times that so many of us can be wrong on a regular basis and not be embarrassed about it. As a society, we seem to be far more interested in the confident assertion of an opinion than in whether that opinion turns out to be right. We love the cocky black-and-white declarations of politicians, movie stars, columnists, activists, bloggers, and just about anybody else with a soapbox to stand on.

In 2011, some people who appear to be genuine Christians honestly thought the world was going to end. They came to this conclusion because they relied on an interpretation of Scripture taught to them by a Bible teacher named Harold Camping. Camping, who had been on the radio for 50 years, had an application of his interpretation that led to some sad and crazy stuff. On one hand, Camping put up billboards warning the end of the world, and a lot of his followers quit their jobs, gave away all their possessions, and ended up facing serious disillusionment from their faith when Judgment Day didn't cooperate and show up on schedule (twice). On the other hand, non-Christians watching this spectacle felt they now had lots of new reasons to mock Christianity. I can't blame them.

None of this would have been possible without bad interpretation, coupled with an unspoken belief among many Christians that *the interpretation of Scripture is somebody else's job.*

Before We Move On

Here at the start, let me try to clear up some potential points of confusion. I'm not trying to say that analyzing someone's interpretation and application of Scripture is a simple thing. There are all kinds of sinful motivations bound up in why we do the things we do. None of these sins and errors are anything new:

- We can accept someone else's bad interpretation due to ignorance, confusion, misunderstanding, bad teaching, or simply by suppressing our conscience.
- We can interpret more or less rightly, and then apply wrongly.
- We often engage in a kind of interpretation without even thinking. We just react, based on, "how we are wired."
- We can even choose plain old rebellion and simply reject the authority of some or all of the Bible, but even that is a kind of bad interpretation, because when I reject Scripture, I elevate my own judgment to a place of higher authority than God's Word.

I am also not saying that getting our interpretation right will fix everything, or that right interpretation is the central purpose of Scripture, or that we can reduce Christian faith to whether we are reading a given passage accurately. But I am saying two things:

1. Without good interpretation being a big part of your routine, you cannot live as Jesus calls you to live. Not possible.
2. Interpretation should involve what others tell you and teach you about Scripture, but ending up with good interpretation is ultimately your own responsibility.

The next four chapters of this book will therefore try to make one point:

Interpretation of Scripture, followed by right application, is the primary way that we are to be like God. This is not an issue of education. It's an issue of imitation.

Jesus demonstrated *how* all believers are to interpret God's Word. We have lost sight of this precious reality and have given its responsibility over to others. Certainly the ongoing teaching of the Scriptures in the church by those called and gifted to do so is absolutely critical. That is, in fact, part of the example Jesus left us. Also, education can be helpful and should not be downplayed or undervalued. I'm simply saying that the pendulum has swung too far, and this has had serious negative implications for everyday believers. Every Christian should be able to interpret most of God's Word simply by following the pattern Jesus left us.

But before we get there, we have to see just how common and how *bad* bad interpretation really is. It is our opposition, and it awaits us.

Two
FROM THE GARDEN TO A GRAINFIELD

A Brief History of Bad Interpretation

In the movie *The Book of Eli*, Denzel Washington plays Eli, a mysterious loner nomad in a world devastated by nuclear war. Eli appears to have been given a book, and he is carrying it across what remains of the United States to a destination only he knows. At one point the book is stolen, and Eli and a younger female companion work to recover it (he gave up on the loner thing for a while – the girl was really pretty). During an intense action scene, Eli risks his life to save the girl. By this point, everyone knows that the mysterious book carried by this mysterious man is the Bible. When he is asked by the girl why he came to save her, Eli replies with what he learned from the Bible. "You gotta do unto others what you want them to do to you. At least, that what I got out of it."

Later in the movie, we realized that Eli has memorized *the entire Bible*. So after committing more than 800,000 words to memory, most of those words hovering tightly around the idea of a sovereign, holy, transcendent God executing his plan to redeem mankind from a fate that would make post-nuclear devastation look like Disney World with no lines and better food, what is Eli's big takeaway truth? What did he "get out of it"? The Golden Rule.

Yeah, yeah, yeah, I know it's just a movie, just Hollywood playing it safe. But in that scene, art is imitating life. It's a sad depiction of how bad everyday interpretation of the Bible often is.

The Origin of Bad Interpretation

Bad interpretation of one kind or another can be seen in all acts of disobedience to the Word of God. And like anything else in creation, bad interpretation had a beginning. In fact, it's as old as mankind. At the beginning of the Bible, we are introduced to bad interpretation. At the end of the Bible, we get a glimpse of what it will be like when all traces of bad interpretation have been scrubbed away and we see and know God for who he truly is. In between, the Bible is busy exposing, confronting, and correcting bad interpretation, and then trying to identify and properly apply good interpretation. You might say that following God in his program of good interpretation and good application is the life's work of every Christian.

The stakes are high. From Adam and Eve to Harold Camping, the consequences of bad interpretation have been catastrophic. Scripture gives us explicit details of the catastrophe, with enough evidence to put bad interpretation on trial for its life. The worst of these acts is the first of these acts – mankind's greatest and most tragic act of misinterpretation.

> Now the serpent was more crafty than any other beast of the field that the LORD God had made. He said to the woman, "Did God actually say, 'You shall not eat of any tree in the garden'?" And the woman said to the serpent, "We may eat of the fruit of the trees in the garden, but God said, 'You shall not eat of the fruit of the tree that is in the midst of the garden, neither shall you touch it, lest you die.'" But the serpent said to the woman, "You will not surely die. For God knows that when you eat of it your eyes will be opened, and you will be like God, knowing good and evil." So when the woman saw that the tree was good for food, and that it was a delight to the eyes, and that the tree was to be desired to make one wise, she took of its fruit and ate, and she also gave some to her husband who was with her, and he ate. (Genesis 3:1-6)

Your interpretation controls how you live. The question that lingers in everybody's heart – *What's the meaning of life?* – is a question about authoritative interpretation. Before sin came into the world, you might say that the interpretive grid through which life should be viewed came completely from God. There was only one source of interpretation. This is what makes Genesis 3 so tragic but also so interesting, because when the serpent enters the picture, God is no longer the sole source for interpreting reality.

We don't know how long Adam and Eve lived in the garden as a couple before they committed the first sin. The words move a lot faster than the events unfolded. Only God knows the timeframe, but we all know the outcome – the first time in the Bible we hear mankind interpreting God's words, they get it tragically wrong. Bad interpretation changed the course of human existence forever. God was no longer mankind's controlling reality, so he was no longer the go-to source of interpretation.

In this passage, there are essentially two interpretations: God's and Eve's, which was influenced by Satan. God's is holy, clear, accurate, and straightforward, while Eve's is sinful, self-serving, imprecise, and layered.

<u>Satan begins by focusing Eve on an interpretive question:</u> "Did God actually say, 'You shall not eat of any tree in the garden'?"

<u>Eve responds by misquoting God.</u> This was the first instance of bad interpretation. Eve claims that "God said, 'You shall not eat of the fruit of the tree that is in the midst of the garden, neither shall you touch it, lest you die.'" The problem is, God never said that exactly. Misquoting may be the most crude and blatant form of misinterpretation, but it is misinterpretation just the same. What God actually said is "You may surely eat of every tree of the garden, but of the tree of the knowledge of good and evil you shall not eat, for in the day that you eat of it you shall surely die" (Genesis 2:16-17). God didn't tell them not to

touch the tree, and he certainly didn't say that touching it *would result in death*, the same penalty as if they ate from it.

Satan comes back with two lies. First, he tempts Adam and Eve's understanding of God's justice. When he says that God would not bring about death as a result of their disobedience, he subtly denies God's authority to punish sin and challenges God's position on what's right and what's wrong.

Satan also raises the stakes by offering the power of independent interpretation. When Satan said, "you will be like God, knowing good and evil," he offered Adam and Eve a false power of interpretation. In street terms, he flunked 'em. He offered them a horrible interpretation of God, knowing that at the very least the consequences would be grave.

It's not clear how much Satan knew about what would happen if they ate the fruit. But it is clear that he knew God. He knew that what God says, God does, yet he offered them a bad interpretation of the Creator and of their role as the created. What is wild is that everything Satan offered to Adam and Eve, they already had. They were *already like God* (he had made them in his image, Genesis 1:26) and they *already had everything they needed to know about good and evil.*

Do you remember what God had said repeatedly about creation? He had declared all of it good. In that garden, it was clear that God was good, his creation was good, and obeying him was good. Anything outside that circle was not good; it was evil.

So Satan tempted Adam and Eve to sin by serving up a dual misinterpretation of what God had spoken: he questioned God's justice, and he questioned the sufficiency of God's definition of good and evil, right and wrong.

There's a lesson here that applies to most instances of interpretation. Adam and Eve trusted not only the serpent's interpretation (of God's words), but also their own interpretation (of Satan's claims). They had to trust *themselves* in determining that *the serpent* was right and God was wrong. They trusted their own ability to choose between one interpretation and another. In fact, before Eve ever reached out for the fruit, man had already assumed the "like God" authority to choose between right and wrong.

Who Gets to Choose?

The first sin was an arrogance of interpretation. Ever since, mankind has suffered a continual plague of arrogance – the arrogance to act on our own view of what's good and what isn't. Adam and Eve chose to take upon themselves a false authority to interpret right from wrong. You and I regularly choose to act on the basis of that same false authority. In a way, we really have become like God, but it's a cheap, shabby imitation.

This issue of authority – what is good, what is evil, and who gets to decide between the two – is a dangerous one. Ultimately what's at stake is a true or a false understanding of God's Word. Whenever we add to or disregard God's Word, we are in essence saying that we have authority over God himself and are the sole arbiters of truth.

Typically, we all interpret and apply to our own benefit. (That's why there are always three sides to every story: your side, my side, and God's side.) When we benefit from our interpretation it is hard to change. Not because change is hard. Change in and of itself is not hard. *Desire to change* is what's hard. Most people don't desire to interpret things differently – they don't want change – if they believe they are benefitting from a wrong interpretation. Like Eve, we believe the serpent's spin. We believe that the consequences of our sinful actions will not be as bad as God has said they will be. It's basically the same deception and the same bad interpretation over and over again.

Our interpretation defines our functional reality. God as Interpreter defined reality for Adam and Eve prior to the Fall. No competing passions, no conflicting purposes. But that grid did not vanish along with Adam and Eve's sinlessness. It still exists, still applies, and still fundamentally affects who we are today. This perfect interpretive grid is not always easy to discern, but it is still Truth. As we will see later in this book, this is why Jesus taught right interpretation and application of God's Word as the primary means to accomplish his mission to save.

Variations on a Theme

Let's learn from a few more examples of bad interpretation. First, we will look at how Saul folded under pressure. Then, we will see how Satan specializes in taking God's

Word out of context. Finally, we will move to Exhibit A, the robed superheroes of bad interpretation, the League of the Extraordinarily Deceived – that's right, the Pharisees.

Saul the King

Chapters 10 through 15 of First Samuel show both the reality of bad interpretation and its consequences. Israel rejects God as their king, preferring someone they can see. They want a king who resembles the rulers of the surrounding nations more than they want to be ruled by the King who created those nations.

God grants their requests and, through the prophet Samuel, chooses Saul. But Saul's obedience would imitate Adam's arrogance. His fall from grace reveals his misinterpretation of that grace.

After Saul is chosen as king, Samuel says these words to him: "Then go down before me to Gilgal. And behold, I am coming to you to offer burnt offerings and to sacrifice peace offerings. Seven days you shall wait, until I come to you and show you what you shall do" (1 Samuel 10:8). These instructions were given in the context of other events which, taken together, proved that Saul had been chosen by God to be the King of Israel, and that God was using Samuel as his spokesman.

For a while, everything is peachy. Saul begins to have great military victories against Israel's most feared opponents. In chapter 13, Saul and his son Jonathan take a small band of soldiers to a Philistine outpost, attack it, and defeat the Philistines easily. The nation of Israel celebrates the victory, gathering around Saul as he blows a horn of triumph. But when the Philistines gather a massive army to retaliate against Israel, the Israelites panic and scatter, every man for himself.

Following Samuel's instructions, Saul goes to Gilgal. He waits there seven days for Samuel, just as he was told. But the seventh day comes and goes, and what Saul expected to happen does not take place: Samuel does not come to offer burnt offerings and peace offerings to God on Saul's behalf. Implicit in those offerings would be God blessing Saul, and thus the nation of Israel in a time of crisis, but Samuel is nowhere to be found and the army of the Philistines approaches like "the sand on the seashore in multitude" (1 Samuel 13:5).

Saul is terrified. He begins rehearsing what the prophet Samuel said he would do. He looks around frantically, hoping Samuel will appear. Seconds feel like hours. The Philistines are ready for an all-out assault against the Jews, and getting so close Saul can almost smell them. Israel's confidence is collapsing, so Saul decides to act.

Saul takes the offerings and presents them to the Lord. As Saul finishes, Samuel approaches, and he is not happy.

> Samuel said, " What have you done?" And Saul said, " When I saw that the people were scattering from me, and that you did not come within the days appointed, and that the Philistines had mustered at Michmash, I said, 'Now the Philistines will come down against me at Gilgal, and I have not sought the favor of the Lord.' So I forced myself, and offered the burnt offering." And Samuel said to Saul, "You have done foolishly.

You have not kept the command of the Lord your God, with which he commanded you. For then the Lord would have established your kingdom over Israel forever." (1 Samuel 13:11-13)

This instance of poorly interpreting God's Word mirrors Genesis 3. Before Saul could come to a place of sin, he had to convince himself that what he was about to do was more right than it was wrong. He had to convince himself that he had a "good reason" for what he was about to do, even though he was clearly going against God's instructions.

We don't know Saul's thoughts exactly. We don't know all the details of his internal struggle. But we do know that he had to force himself to do something that at first seemed like a really bad idea. Saul had come to an interpretation of God's word that opened the door for him to disobey it.

The exact nature of Saul's sin isn't entirely clear. Some say it was connected to 1 Samuel 10:8 and the fact that only priests had the authority to offer those sacrifices to God. Some think it was another command unrecorded in the Bible. Both are possible. In either case, the issue of Saul dismissing Samuel's word to wait for him was bad – so bad that it would cost him his kingship.

Underneath every act of sin is a wrong interpretation of God's Word. And that wrong view led Saul to sin against God. We'll come back to Saul later, but for now let's consider another misinterpretation of God's Word.

Satan

To me, right after Adam and Eve's failure, the second worst display of interpretation in Scripture, and perhaps in history, is Satan tempting Jesus. Yep, that old serpent is back, and in Matthew 4 we see that Satan knows God's Word. He knows it better than you or I or your favorite theologian. He probably has it memorized in every human language, including those that don't even have the Bible yet. And I guarantee you his understanding of it runs a lot deeper than Denzel's Eli character spouting the Golden Rule.

Satan knows the Bible as well as he does not out of reverence for God, but so he can mess with our heads, just like he tried with Jesus in the wilderness. Satan is very good at tempting us with bad interpretations of God's Word, and in Matthew 4, we see how he does it.

This scene is ironic when you take into account who is talking to whom. Satan uses God's Word to try to tempt the very Word of God himself! That's just crazy, but it shows how off the hook our Enemy can be sometimes.

In trying to get Jesus, or us, to interpret God's Word wrongly, one of the biggest wrenches in Satan's toolbox involves taking God's Word out of context. In Matthew 4 we read about Satan making three such efforts to tempt Jesus into sin. In one of these, Satan tries to use Scripture to get Jesus to obey him. Quoting from Psalm 91:11-12, the Devil urges Jesus to throw himself off of the temple:

> Then the devil took him to the holy city and set him
> on the pinnacle of the temple and said to him, "If

you are the Son of God, throw yourself down, for it
is written, 'He will command his angels concerning
you,' and 'On their hands they will bear you up, **lest
you strike your foot against a stone.'"** (Matthew 4:5-6)

Here, Satan reminds Jesus of the Scripture by quoting
it, without taking into account the whole counsel of God.
Jesus is unimpressed, to say the least. Even after 40 days
in the desert without food and water, he still has enough
game to know that Satan is playing to foul.

Because Jesus knows the whole counsel of God, he
exposes Satan's interpretation for what it really is: "Jesus
said to him, 'Again it is written, "You shall not put the
Lord your God to the test"'" (47). Game clock reads
00:00. It's over. The Devil just doesn't know it yet.

Wrong interpretation is all over the pages of Scripture,
but Adam, Eve, Saul, and Satan are just a few of the
culprits. There is a lot more room on the bad interpretation train, and the Pharisees are walking the aisles
collecting tickets stubs.

The Pharisees

Throughout the earthly life of Jesus, no one had the
interpretation of God's Word more backwards than
the Pharisees. These were the pastors of their day (no
offense – I'm a pastor myself). They were highly respected
and often feared, and they seemed to crave both responses.
The Pharisees were supposedly the "Back to the Bible"
guys, but they ended up going far beyond the Bible.

These men had been entrusted to interpret and

explain God's Word. Each week in the Synagogue, Pharisees would read and interpret the Law and the Prophets to the children of Abraham. They would take a text, read it aloud, and offer some perspective on it. But the legacy of the Pharisees is that the perspective they offered on Scripture ended up becoming a set of legalistic rules. Then, in effect, the Pharisees turned those rules around and used them to reinterpret Scripture, so that the typical Israelite understood the Bible to be all about legalism.

That same tendency to look at the Bible, interpret it wrongly, then pivot back around and see Scripture in the light of your own false interpretation is at the heart of the legalism that has plagued God's people from the very beginning.

The Law of Moses was given *by* God to reveal humanity's inability to *obey* God. The way the Israelites throughout their history had consistently turned away from God rather than to him was a proof-positive, spiritual DNA match proving their guilt. Rebellion became the Israelites' identity. Judgment became their daily condition.

What's astonishing is that the Pharisees didn't get this at all. The ones who had been entrusted to interpret the Old Testament to the people for whom it was written completely failed to grasp the fundamental underlying point. (Which, ironically, only further proves that point.)

Not only did the Pharisees believe it possible to keep the Law, they thought it was an act of faithfulness to God to add more rules to it! Even worse, these men had the amazing talent of telling others what to do without doing it themselves. In addition to interpreting much of the Mosaic law badly, the Pharisees went a step further and pretended other parts of the law just weren't there. Bad interpretation combined with selective observation and application put these men in a league of hypocrisy all by themselves. When Jesus came, he took a look at that league and decided to call some new plays. He didn't just change the rules. He changed the whole game.

Here was a group of men in control of telling God's chosen people how they should read and interpret and obey the Word of God. They managed to construct a system that exalted themselves, oppressed the people, misrepresented God, obscured the truth of the Scriptures, and locked out any possibility of opposition. No wonder Jesus was out to expose them.

Not surprisingly, given the role of the Pharisees as supposed Keepers of Truth, the conflicts Jesus had with them were fundamentally about interpretation. Actions come from understanding. Application follows interpretation. The Pharisees knew this as well as Jesus did. So the fundamental conflict between them was that the Pharisees expected Jesus to act more like them, and Jesus expected the Pharisees to act more like God.

The specific conflicts that Jesus had with the Pharisees can seem distant to us because we're not from the culture of second-temple Judaism. At times I have had no idea what Jesus and the Pharisees are talking about. It's hard to relate to the details of their arguments, but it's easy to relate to the underlying battle of interpretation.

Matthew 12:1-14 contains two great examples. In each case, the question of interpretation involves what is lawful to do on the Sabbath and what isn't. But the real issue is who has the authority to interpret Scripture and how and why. It's obvious here that Jesus is setting up opportunities for the Pharisees to make their case for legalism so that he can then turn around and speak truth into the situation.

Here are the two questions addressed in this passage:

- If you are walking through a grainfield on the Sabbath, does the Mosaic law permit you to pluck some heads of grain and eat as you walk along?
- If someone is suffering physically, and it's the Sabbath, does the Mosaic law give you permission to try to make the person better?

The Pharisees thought the answer to both questions was no. But they didn't base their answer to either question on what the Mosaic law actually said about the Sabbath specifically or what it taught about the nature and purpose of the Sabbath generally. Jesus does, though. He mentions a few Old Testament passages and throws in a bomb about how he has all authority over the Sabbath anyway. Jesus is the great interpreter. He gets to the heart of God's Word.

But that wasn't good enough for the Pharisees. Maybe they worried that they would fail miserably at keeping God's law, or maybe they really thought they understood God's law better than anyone else, so they drew up lists that "explained" what people must or must not do in order to be righteous. The Pharisees' interpretation became, in effect, the "word of God" because it was what people believed God wanted them to do, while the actual Word of God was set aside.

Preparing to Meet the Interpreter

Have you ever wondered why the Gospels give so much attention to the Pharisees? Is it so whenever Christians get together we can talk about how bad they were without actually gossiping? I don't think so. The New Testament lessons about the Pharisees are so we can take to heart the fact that we are not very different from them.

Interpretation is how we do life every moment of every day. The most important kind of interpretation is what we understand the content, authority, and purpose of the Bible to be, and therefore who we understand God to be. But just like the Pharisees, *we can all tend to rely on our interpretation of those things more than we rely on the Bible itself.*

Interpretation is not the same as knowing what the Bible says. As part of their training, the Pharisees committed to memory much of the Old Testament, and they still got it horribly wrong. In failing to understand the Old Testament accurately, the Pharisees failed to understand God accurately – and this, ultimately, is the greatest danger of false interpretation.

Like a TV weatherman who has been consistently wrong for the last month but still comes on air with a big smile and lots of confidence, we can act like self-assured dummies about our interpretation of Scripture. But we don't have to do that any longer. Despite all the bad interpretation everywhere around us, there is room to rejoice. The Son of God, the Interpreter himself, has come, and he teaches us how to interpret his Word correctly. We do not need to be in theological darkness about the Bible. The interpretive grid that was lost in the Garden of Eden is still available to us. God the Son has come that we might regain a right understanding of God, a right relationship to God, and right interpretation of his holy Word.

Three
JESUS THE INTERPRETER

Interpretation Is More about Imitation than Education

Right interpretation of God's Word is difficult but doable. More than that, it is an expectation of God for his people and a process as old as the origins of Scripture itself.

To give us the Old and New Testaments, God inspired men to write down his Word. The writing process itself inevitably involved a certain amount of (divinely inspired) interpretation, and the words that were written included no small number of commands from God that we apply, or obey, that Word. This tells us that the entire paradigm of right interpretation leading to right application is an essential, foundational gift from God to his people. So much so that this gift ultimately came in the form of a person named Jesus, the Christ.

Have you ever wondered why Jesus is called the Word of God? Out of all the things that the Son of God could have been described as, why the Word? Why does the Creator of the universe come to us as the living, breathing Word of God? There are several ways to answer these questions, and this book is too short to get into them all, but let's consider a few.

John 1 tells us some interesting things about Jesus. "In the beginning was the Word, and the Word was with God, and the Word was God.... And the Word became flesh and dwelt among us, and we have seen his glory" (vv 1, 14).

What is obvious is that Jesus, since the beginning, has been the Word of God who *is* God. The Greek word that John uses here is *Logos*, meaning *word* or *speech*. We know that God has no beginning, so "in the beginning" is a temporal reference point for time-bound creatures, something to help us process the significance of Jesus' identity: unlike anything else, Jesus *has been* since, well, forever. It also reminds us that Jesus was and is the sustainer of all creation.

The Word of God is life and creates life. The Word has no end, just as it had no beginning. The Word of God is the enemy of death and will defeat death. It's all rather poetic and mysterious, I know, but how does Jesus being this Word connect to our discussion of interpretation?

To answer that question, we must remember that all things were created through the Word. Genesis tells us that the sun, the birds of the air, and the plants of the field were spoken into existence. These all came into being by God's Word, and they are sustained by that same Word. In their day-to-day activities they do not interact with that Word except to simply respond. There is no conscious questioning or resistance because *they make no interpretation*.

But once God created man, something new entered the picture: interpretation became possible, and with it came the possibility of false interpretation as well as conscious defiance, refusal, rebellion, and rejection. Unlike with the rest of the natural world, God granted man free will, and free will requires an ability to interpret and evaluate and weigh and choose – not just respond according to natural laws or instinct.

Interpreters of the Alpha and Omega

We are made in God's image. We are made to think and interpret. We are the only earthly creature that interprets God's words. We hear them, we think about their meaning, and we act on the basis of our thoughts and conclusions.

This is critical to understanding Jesus as being the *Logos*, or Word, of John 1. We are interpreters *by God's design*, so the highest and most significant acts of interpretation we engage in are our interpretations of God's Word. In the New Testament Age, this puts Jesus – the Word of God – front and center as our principal object of interpretation. We interpret who Jesus is, what he has said, and what his words mean, and then we determine how we will respond to our interpretations.

Prior to the Incarnation, the principal focus of interpretation was God's written and spoken Word. In Genesis 3 that Word was misinterpreted and misapplied. This brought sin *into* the world. Today, the Word of God rightly interpreted and rightly applied is the only thing that will take sinners safely *out of* this world.

You might say, then, that John 1 is simply Genesis 1's better half. It's an eternal do-over, a re-presentation of

43

truth and another chance for mankind to interpret God's Word accurately and to act accordingly. Genesis set in motion a series of events that would lead to the Mosaic law, but John 1 revisits those same beginnings to reveal Christ in them, ultimately leading to something far better: salvation through Jesus the Word. John shows us the larger package in which God's plan was enclosed: Jesus the Word, the beginning and end of creation, the first and the last.

Jesus the Interpreter and Object of Scripture

Jesus is also the primary interpreter of Scripture because he is the primary object of Scripture. Jesus alone knows what all Scripture means because it is about him. While on earth, Jesus preached a message of repentance and belief in himself. He was not shy or inaccurate about who he was, what he was doing, or why he was doing it.

As I said in chapter 1, we could boil the focus of Jesus' life down to evangelism and discipleship, both of which he accomplishes by communicating accurate interpretation and urging right application of God's Word. This reality is often dismissed when it comes to *imitating what Jesus did*, but some of the most amazing things recorded in Scripture are not actual miracles but the instances when God explains his own Word to people and then shows them how to apply it. This is the pattern of Christian discipleship, and one of the primary ways in which we should imitate our Lord. Interpretation and application of God's Word is of the highest importance to Jesus.

In almost every instance where we see Jesus interpreting God's written Word, he quotes the Scriptures, explains the Scriptures, and then offers application. In Matthew 5, during the famous Sermon on the Mount, Jesus interprets and applies God's Word by stepping through this entire process five times, beginning at verses 21, 27, 33, 38, and 43. In each case, his basic launching point for bringing together the worlds of interpretation and application is the phrase, "You have heard that it was said":

> You have heard that it was said, "You shall not commit adultery." But I say to you that everyone who looks at a woman with lustful intent has already committed adultery with her in his heart. If your right eye causes you to sin, tear it out and throw it away. For it is better that you lose one of your members than that your whole body be thrown into hell. And if your right hand causes you to sin, cut it off and throw it away. For it is better that you lose one of your members than that your whole body go into hell. (Matthew 5:27-30)

> What is happening here?

- Verse 27: Jesus quotes God's Word.
- Verse 28: Jesus rightly interprets God's Word.
- Verse 29-30 : Jesus gives application of God's Word.

This pattern was vital to Jesus' earthly ministry. As we are called to be imitators of God, we must consider that rightly interpreting God's Word is an essential element of that call – whether we are educated in theology or not.

In Matthew 5:17 Jesus identifies the reason he can even make these "you have heard it was said" statements: "Do not think that I have come to abolish the Law or the Prophets; I have not come to abolish them but to fulfill them." Jesus is clear. He came to fulfill the Law. Because he is the primary object of the Law, by default he is also the primary interpreter of that Law.

Requirements for Understanding Scripture

Let's notice something in the life and ministry of Jesus specifically and the Word of God generally: formal training *in* God's Word is never set forth as a requirement for accurate understanding *of* God's Word. Indeed, most of the people with formal training rejected Jesus in his day. Even among Christians, training in theology does not necessarily lead to genuine affection for God or even to good application. Heart knowledge does not necessarily follow from head knowledge.

An unspoken message in the evangelical world is that formal training of some kind – be it Bible college or seminary or something else – is necessary if we want to have an accurate understanding of God's Word. But when we look *at* God's Word, the only requirements seem to be faith and the indwelling of God's Holy Spirit. The foreshadowing of the New Covenant presented in Jeremiah 31:33-34 says as much:

> For this is the covenant that I will make with the house of Israel after those days, declares the Lord: I will put

my law within them, and I will write it on their hearts. And I will be their God, and they shall be my people. And no longer shall each one teach his neighbor and each his brother, saying, "Know the Lord," for they shall all know me, from the least of them to the greatest, declares the Lord. For I will forgive their iniquity, and I will remember their sin no more.

This is a description of everyone who is in Christ. We can interpret God's Word enough to live in wonderful relationship with him. All without formal training! Don't get me wrong. I do believe that training in theological studies is immensely helpful, especially if you are called to be a teacher of God's Word. However, we have lost sight of a fundamental truth about *how we are all to be like Jesus*. We have made interpretation far more about education than imitation, which doesn't seem to be God's intention or his requirement. The New Testament example of the Bereans certainly indicates that every Christian needs to take the Scriptures with the utmost seriousness (Acts 17:11), but checking up on what you have been taught is one thing, while a prolonged process of formal education is something else altogether.

All Christians are called to be readers and interpreters, evangelists and disciplers. And right interpretation of the Word is fundamental to it all.

This is why Jesus inquired often about people's reading habits.

Have You Not Read?

When Jesus was asked questions about life – about application – he often responded, "Have you not read?" In Matthew 12, verses 3-8 in particular, after the Pharisees accuse Jesus and his disciples of breaking the Sabbath, Jesus questions the Pharisees' answers by bringing them back to their bad interpretation of God's Word:

> Have you not read what David did when he was hungry, and those who were with him: how he entered the house of God and ate the bread of the Presence, which it was not lawful for him to eat nor for those who were with him, but only for the priests? Or have you not read in the Law how on the Sabbath the priests in the temple profane the Sabbath and are guiltless? I tell you, something greater than the temple is here. And if you had known what this means, "I desire mercy, and not sacrifice," you would not have condemned the guiltless. For the Son of Man is lord of the Sabbath.

What do we see here? For our sake, for the sake of his disciples there that day, and for the sake of the Pharisees themselves, Jesus is exposing the weaknesses of the Pharisees' view of Scripture by presenting an accurate view of Scripture. He does this by providing insight in four areas – two involving the Law and two involving God. We will look at that insight as answers to four questions:

- What does it mean for something to be unlawful?
- What makes something unlawful on the Sabbath?
- What would be a right view of God relative to the Sabbath?
- What is God's relationship to the Sabbath?

Jesus addresses the Pharisees' interpretation of God's Word about the Sabbath by going directly at their application. He uses two illustrations, one from Israel's history and another from what happens in the temple every Sabbath.

Here it comes. A front row seat to watch and learn how to be better interpreters, and at the Pharisees' expense.

What Does It Mean for Something to Be Unlawful?

He said to them, "Have you not read what David did when he was hungry, and those who were with him: how he entered the house of God and ate the bread of the Presence, which it was not lawful for him to eat nor for those who were with him, but only for the priests?" (Matthew 12:3-4)

The first illustration Jesus offers takes them back more than 1000 years to David in 1 Samuel 21:1-6.

Jonathan had informed David that Saul – Jonathan's father, the current King of Israel – was going to try to kill him (1 Samuel 20), so David fled for his life to Nob. He went into the Tabernacle there and found Ahimelech,

Saul's priest, whom he asked for bread. The only bread available was the Bread of Presence, which was consecrated bread, usually twelve loaves, set out in the Holy Place as a thank offering to God. Each loaf represented one of the twelve tribes of Israel; together the loaves were symbolic of Israel's covenantal relationship with God. Every Sabbath the loaves were replaced with fresh ones, and the priests ate the old loaves. The bread was considered holy and was reserved for "Aaron and his sons" – that is, those in the priesthood. But David was not a priest, and neither were his men.

Technically, therefore, eating the bread of the Presence was a clear violation of the ceremonial portion of the Mosaic law, and it certainly would have violated the Pharisaical interpretation of the law in Jesus' day. Jesus himself acknowledged this. Yet it does not appear that at the time God was displeased. More significantly, Jesus openly approved of it.

Human need apparently takes precedence over ritual custom. If David and Ahimelech were allowed to ignore a divinely ordained ceremonial provision in the face of particular circumstances, then Jesus, God incarnate, certainly had the same basic right.

By starting with "have you not read," Jesus speaks directly to the pride of the Pharisees' interpretation. These supposed authorities on God's Word completely missed the point of 1 Samuel 20, which they had, in fact, read many, many times. What is that point? That ceremonial restrictions can be ousted in the face of necessity. David and Ahimelech made right application of the Mosaic law regarding the Tabernacle, and it became recorded in Scripture as a lesson in application. But the Pharisees missed it, and their bad interpretation led to bad application, which formed the basis of their accusation that Jesus' disciples were violating the law as they plucked and fed themselves a few grains of wheat on the Sabbath day.

What Makes Something Unlawful on the Sabbath?

"Or have you not read in the Law how on the Sabbath the priests in the temple profane the Sabbath and are guiltless?" (Matthew 12:5)

Jesus' second illustration here reemphasizes the importance of right interpretation of God's Word. He begins with the same question, "Have you not read?" but this time, Jesus is referring to the Sabbath duty of the priests. (By "profane the temple" he means actions devoted to that which is not sacred or biblical, actions that are more secular than they are religious.)

Because offerings in the temple were doubled on the Sabbath (see Numbers 28:9-10), it was by far the roughest day of the week for the priests – nothing even close to a day of rest. And the work they were doing was, in fact, how they made a living. Technically, therefore, the priests broke Sabbath rules every Sabbath! But from God's perspective, the temple worship of God took precedence, which is the same lesson given in 1 Samuel 21. The priests broke the Law, yet they were guiltless, because serving people in need is more important than rules about rituals.

What Would Be a Right View of God Relative to the Sabbath?

"I tell you, something greater than the temple is here."
(Matthew 12:6)

Here, Jesus basically says: "So you guys are big on the sanctity of temple worship? Then have I got news for you." The "something" of which Jesus spoke – something greater than the temple – was himself. His point was that if regulations pertaining to the temple could be set aside in cases of necessity, how much more could they be set aside in the presence of someone greater than the temple?

So Jesus begins to correct the Pharisees' view of God. It's not clear they understood that Jesus was referring to himself as "greater than the temple." Maybe they just didn't care. In any event, with this statement, Jesus begins a theological shift. He began by discussing Sabbath rules, but he now moves to the Sabbath ruler. Jesus will address the Pharisees' view *of* God by stating the reality that he himself *is* God. Once again, he exposes wrongly applied interpretation (bad theology) simply by rightly interpreting Scripture.

Jesus corrects the Pharisees' interpretation of God's Word because that was where their error began, leading to bad application. But we also see that both their interpretation and their application shaped what they thought God was like. Because the Pharisees were the teachers of their day, their view of God tended to become the people's view of God, and it was way off the mark. Just like today, where people trust pastors to unpack the Scriptures for them and trust their application without thinking about the Scriptures themselves, the Pharisees carried on their shoulders a great weight of responsibility, and they were not carrying it well.

This is why Jesus goes on to make a powerful statement about what God is really like.

What Is God's Relationship to the Sabbath?

"And if you had known what this means, 'I desire mercy, and not sacrifice,' you would not have condemned the guiltless. For the Son of Man is lord of the Sabbath." (Matthew 12:7-8)

The Pharisees *fundamentally believe that God is like them.* In all their harsh legalism, they believe they are acting consistent with the will and character of God. So Jesus, again, appeals to the Word of God to reinterpret for them what God is really like. "I desire mercy and not sacrifice," is a quotation from Hosea 6:6. Such scriptural references may seem subtle to us, but Jesus knows they speak loudly and clearly to the Pharisees.

Whenever Jesus quotes the Old Testament to the Pharisees, he is showing them where their interpretation and application fall short. Here he is essentially saying: "You think God is like you but you are wrong. God is merciful and therefore he places acts of mercy above acts of sacrifice. God desires that men who are hungry eat rather than starve. God doesn't condemn the guiltless. To understand God, and to apply that understanding, is to show mercy to others."

From the very beginning, God's mercy has been clearly displayed. He spared Adam and Eve from the full and immediate application of his wrath, giving them and all of us the opportunity to turn to him and be saved. In fact, God's response to the first sin is an act of mercy and kindness: "And the Lord God made for Adam and for his wife garments of skins and clothed them" (Genesis 3:21).

Even in the Law, with all of its rules, God still provided a means to display his mercy toward all who fail to keep the Law – the Day of Atonement in Leviticus 16. This is a merciful God. He is not like the legalistic Pharisees, harsh, self-righteous, and unappeasable. And that merciful Lord had come on the scene to confront the Pharisees in their unmerciful legalism.

Jesus ends this section by describing himself, in verse 8, as lord of the Sabbath. The "something" referenced in verse 6 as being greater than the temple has become a Someone. There is a stairway to Jesus' presentation to the Pharisees here, and we are now at the top of it.

When Jesus says to the Pharisees "the Son of Man is lord of the Sabbath," it is not clear that they immediately got his point. Although there are a number of levels to Jesus' statement, for our immediate purposes I will just emphasize this: Jesus is saying that God is not *bound* by any human interpretation of the Law, and certainly not by the view of the Pharisees. Jesus interprets and applies Sabbath law according to himself. He is not constrained by the Sabbath because he is above the Sabbath. He alone knows what the Sabbath means and how it should be applied.

First Things First

Through Matthew 12 we can begin to see the pattern of
Jesus' interpretative grid. Jesus knows the whole counsel
of God. He knows how it all connects. That knowledge is
the lens through which all believers must learn to interpret
God's Word. Again, it does not require seminary training.
Jesus isn't focusing anyone on schooling. He doesn't
adjust the Pharisees' interpretation by giving them study
hints or chiding them for not working hard enough.

Instead, Jesus corrects their incapacity to believe.
Their interpretation of God affected a whole nation's
obedience to God. Millions of people had been subject to
bad application because of bad interpretation. Yet, in the
midst of that, there were still those who trusted God in
faith. From the evidence of the New Testament it appears
that most of those people were not educated.

Education has never been the standard. It is certainly
not irrelevant, but the testimony of Scripture is that
education takes its place behind imitation of God. Only
when education and imitation are in proper relationship
can we move on to application. Right application follows
right interpretation, and in the following chapter we will
see this demonstrated in the life of Jesus.

The greatest and most significant interpretation that
Jesus the Word has ever given is his interpretation of God.
He showed us that God is not a mean dispenser of rules
but a merciful protector, standard-bearer, and redeemer.
Yet the Savior does more than just explain who God is and
what God meant: he shows us how to live in a right interpretation of God. You cannot imitate what you do not

understand. Jesus is making sure that we do understand. A s he does, we should imitate him.

Four
FROM INTERPRETATION TO APPLICATION

Jesus, the Pharisees and the Sabbath

We have seen Jesus interpret Scripture through his words. Now, as we move on in Matthew 12, we will see Jesus interpret Scripture by his actions – applying to real-life situations the implications of proper biblical interpretation. In this instance, he does this by directly challenging the Pharisees' actual understanding of the Sabbath and its purpose.

> He went on from there and entered their synagogue. And a man was there with a withered hand. And they asked him, "Is it lawful to heal on the Sabbath?" – so that they might accuse him. He said to them, "Which one of you who has a sheep, if it falls into a pit on the Sabbath, will not take hold of it and lift it out? Of how much more value is a man than a sheep! So it is lawful to do good on the Sabbath." Then he said

to the man, "Stretch out your hand." And the man
stretched it out, and it was restored, healthy like the
other. (Matthew 12:9-13)

Jesus goes into the Synagogue, and the Pharisees,
still believing that they have the right interpretation of
Sabbath law, try yet again to accuse him. In verse 10 their
question reveals their motive. Jesus responds and, through
his words and actions, makes an astonishing claim about
the Sabbath. The Pharisees' question is meant to trap Jesus,
but when he interprets Sabbath law for them, he reveals
God's intention for the Sabbath, and he therefore reveals
that he's the only one in the room who really understands
God's Word.

This was not the first public clash between Jesus and
the Pharisees. In fact, most of their clashes happened in
public. This particular scene is set in the synagogue, a very
holy and a very public place. It's safe to assume that others
in the temple at the same time knew something about this
rivalry between the Pharisees – the entrenched authorities – and this astonishing newcomer who had an amazing
ability *not* to play by the rules but still to seem blameless.
So when the Pharisees asked, "Is it lawful to heal on the
Sabbath?" it must have been quiet enough to hear animals
eating a few miles away.

Scripture doesn't give us the tone of the Pharisees'
question, but it does give us the heart of the questioners.
You don't need much imagination to see how indignant
the question probably sounded. Remember, this is the
same day as the Sabbath questions about grain and the

Bread of the Presence. The last thing Jesus said to the Pharisees before he entered the synagogue was, "The Son of Man is lord of the Sabbath." The Pharisees probably saw this as first-century trash talk because Jesus was basically accusing them of being clueless about an area where they were supposed to be the reigning experts. Now here they are with Jesus again, this time in the synagogue, almost certainly feeling offended, indignant, and threatened.

The question they pose is not based in curiosity. It is based in animosity. The other Jews in the synagogue were probably holding their breath and glancing at each other in fear.

Earlier in the day, Jesus verbally refuted the Pharisaical interpretation of Sabbath law, but now he rightly *applies* Sabbath law. By appealing to a situation that would not be unusual on the Sabbath, he exposes the Pharisees' bad exegesis or interpretation.

The Law of Mercy

> *He said to them, "Which one of you who has a sheep, if it falls into a pit on the Sabbath, will not take hold of it and lift it out?"* (Matthew 12:11)

Jesus' question reveals the Pharisees' hypocrisy. They *would* do what they considered unlawful on the Sabbath if it were *their* animal in the pit. More concerning is that the Pharisees' interpretation of the Sabbath led them to think that animals are more important than people. (PETA may owe the Pharisees a debt of gratitude on this point.)

Jesus' question began to make clear that these self-righteous religious leaders acted as if healing a man on the Sabbath glorifies God less than grabbing a sheep from a pit does. Which is really odd if you know anything about sheep.

I must confess that I am a city boy. Only once have I been really close to a sheep, and I remember two things about that experience. I was a believer by then, so I remember being emotionally affected by the way God uses sheep as a metaphor in Scripture. I remember thinking about Jesus being the Lamb of God. I also remember thinking that we are all just sheep, and that wolves sometimes come in to try and rip the sheep apart. I can't capture the emotion of that moment in words, but it definitely had a profound effect on me.

My other impression was less philosophical. I remember how *big* the sheep were. Maybe not all sheep grow to that size, but these had to weigh a couple hundred pounds, easy. They looked like big, dusty cotton balls running into a wooden fence. A guy walked over and asked if I wanted to pick one up and I looked at him like he had asked if he could borrow a few thousand dollars. Even with the imagery of the Savior as a lamb fresh in my mind, I'm not so sentimental that I wanted to pick one up. Not to mention that the one the dude pointed to looked like a buffalo sheep. That thing was big! Maybe he thought that because I'm a big dude I could probably handle it. But my mind went immediately to the TV show *When Animals Attack*. All I could imagine was a videotape being shown around the world of that sheep hoofing the mess out of my face. No sir! Let me admire from afar.

So if the sheep Jesus is referring to were anywhere near the size of the ones I saw that day, then absolutely it would have been a lot of work to grab one from a ditch. The Pharisees' hypocrisy was obvious. It takes much more work to pull a sheep from a ditch than for Jesus to heal a man's hand. Even so, the amount of work was not Jesus' primary concern. Instead, he wanted to point out the *comparative value* of the creature being helped.

"Of how much more value is a man than a sheep!" Jesus said in verse 12, "So it is lawful to do good on the Sabbath." The main point Jesus wanted to make here is that ethical conduct is always more important than ceremonial obedience. It was hard for the Pharisees to see this. Under their interpretation and application of the Law, rituals had become greater than mercy and greater than love. They were so deep in their bad interpretation that they had long ago lost clarity on what it really means to honor the Lord.

Let's look at that moment at the end of verse 12 when Jesus has stopped speaking but hasn't yet acted. What do you suppose the response was to Jesus' point about the value of a man versus a sheep? I'm guessing Jesus spoke those words and then stopped and looked at the Pharisees for a minute, just waiting. And I'm guessing his gaze was met by a long, awkward pause as everyone else glanced back and forth between Jesus and the Pharisees.

No one waited with more anticipation than the man whose hand needed healing.

It's not clear how long the man's hand had been withered, but Jesus' fame had been spreading for a while. The man probably knew that if Jesus calls you out, unless you're a religious leader or a tax collector, it's probably a good thing. So in my view the room is filled at that moment by a tense, dead silence. All the man can hear is his own heartbeat, Jesus' question to the Pharisees reverberating through the synagogue, and those animals eating a few miles away.

These Pharisees were either stumped or too stubborn to acknowledge that Jesus is right. Can you see why Jesus is angry with them? They created a rigid set of self-righteous laws, and they believed that God was like them. No wonder they didn't recognize Jesus! They were looking for a harsh, self-righteous, sinner-hating Messiah – someone who would honor their piety and eject from the temple anyone unworthy to worship there. They were wrong, and their sin is our lesson: bad interpretation will lead to bad application. If they had paid attention to Jesus, they would have learned how to interpret accurately, which would have led to them act rightly. They would have understood mercy.

Mercy Applied

Then he said to the man, "Stretch out your hand."
And the man stretched it out, and it was restored,
healthy like the other. (Matthew 12:13)

Right interpretation leads to right application. It really is lawful to do good on the Sabbath.

What can easily go unnoticed here is how the man's hand was healed. Jesus didn't touch him. He didn't actually do any work. Technically, he did nothing to heal the guy - no surgery, no incantations, no rubbing oils, nothing. In one sense he didn't even break the Pharisees' interpretation of Sabbath law because all he actually did was say to the man, "Stretch out your hand."

Yet, as Jesus the Word spoke, reality was altered, just like at Creation. The man's hand was miraculously healed. I believe Jesus did all this very intentionally. The Pharisees were accusing Jesus of breaking God's law, so Jesus - the lord of the Sabbath - healed the man in a way that only God could. Like the rest of Jesus' miracles, this one was proof of his claim to be the Son of God. Through these supernatural displays of mercy, God's glory was supposed to be celebrated by all who witnessed the events.

The healing in that synagogue was clearly from God. It was also indisputable evidence that the Son of Man is lord of the Sabbath. Everyone, including the Pharisees, should have rejoiced to see God working in their midst. Unfortunately, the Pharisees couldn't see past what they thought Jesus was doing wrong. Had they been more interested in Scripture and less interested in the rules they had added to Scripture, they might have seen that Jesus was demonstrating what God is really like.

Interpreting the Sabbath Rest

Remember how we learned in chapter 2 that the Pharisees made checklists for God's law? They had a list of 39 activities that they claimed were forbidden on the Sabbath.

Matthew 12:1-14 is about activities allowed by the Mosaic law but forbidden by the Pharisees' bad interpretation of that Law. Because they taught these rules regularly and rigidly, the Israelites completely lost the purpose of the Sabbath – to gratefully remember God as provider of all things – and replaced it with a lingering fear that you might be breaking Rule 37 … or was it Rule 19?

Jesus' actions in Matthew 12 represent right application based on right interpretation, specifically of the Fourth Commandment, the one pertaining to the Sabbath. Let's look again at the two key Old Testament passages setting forth the Sabbath command:

> Remember the Sabbath day, to keep it holy. Six days you shall labor, and do all your work, but the seventh day is a Sabbath to the LORD your God. On it you shall not do any work, you, or your son, or your daughter, your male servant, or your female servant, or your livestock, or the sojourner who is within your gates. For in six days the LORD made heaven and earth, the sea, and all that is in them, and rested on the seventh day. Therefore the LORD blessed the Sabbath day and made it holy. (Exodus 20:8-11)

> Observe the Sabbath day, to keep it holy, as the LORD your God commanded you. Six days you shall labor and do all your work, but the seventh day is a Sabbath to the LORD your God. On it you shall not do any work, you or your son or your daughter or your male servant or your female servant, or your ox or your

> donkey or any of your livestock, or the sojourner
> who is within your gates, that your male servant and
> your female servant may rest as well as you. You shall
> remember that you were a slave in the land of Egypt,
> and the LORD your God brought you out from
> there with a mighty hand and an outstretched arm.
> Therefore the LORD your God commanded you to
> keep the Sabbath day. (Deuteronomy 5:12-15)

The Sabbath is about rest. From the beginning, God created mankind to be mirror images of his mercy, goodness, and faithfulness. Although sin obviously changed our ability to do this flawlessly, it never changed God's intent. Theologically, rest is part of how God helps us do what he made us to do; it represents a reversal of the chaotic infiltration of sin. To a significant degree, Sabbath rest is about a return to the Garden of Eden, to a state of peace. This kind of rest is a destination – the end goal for all of God's people who believe.

When God chose Israel to be his people, he told them they would leave Egypt for Canaan to receive *rest*. For them, the Sabbath was about imitating God who rested from work on the seventh day. Whenever they thought of Sabbath, they thought of rest. On the Sabbath day, the whole nation should rest.

The Pharisees wrongly interpreted the Sabbath rest to mean avoiding nearly all activity. They saw rest the way teenagers often do – doing nothing. But it appears that the Sabbath law had in mind a specific kind of activity that constituted real rest.

Look closely at the work that Exodus 20 refers to. Verse 9 talks about doing "your work" six days a week. Then verse 10 names the different categories of people and animals that should not work on the Sabbath. These verses point to a specific kind of work – work that earns wages. The main focus here is any labor that constitutes making a living.

The Sabbath is the one day that the Jews were to rest from *the work that earns* in order to remember *the God who provides.* When God rested in Genesis 2:1-2 he rested from working after seeing that what he had done was good. He then set aside a day so that man, whom he would create in his image, could reflect on that good.

Deuteronomy 5 indicates that Israel was to use the Sabbath to reflect on having been freed from bondage in Egypt. It was not a day of inactivity but a day of worship and reflection on the God of their salvation. Even today, we as God's people need that reflection. In all the hustle and bustle of life, it can be easy to forget about God. It's easy to get caught up in various things and end up not reading your Bible or meditating on how good God has been in saving you by his grace.

The Pharisees interpreted the references to labor in these passages as meaning that we should cease activity in general. Yet nowhere in Scripture do you see God inactive in this way. Rest from God's perspective is not the absence of activity. All things are sustained in and through God (Hebrews 1:3), so if God rested from all activity on the seventh day, everything would cease to exist every week! We would have six days of activity and then nothing. God would have to create everything all over again, the same creation week repeated forever.

God is clearly no fan of inactivity. He is the one who instituted work as central to man's role even before the Fall (see Genesis 2:15). Therefore, slothfulness is disparaged in Scripture (see Proverbs 19:24). Paul rebuked those in the church who refused to work (2 Thessalonians 3:6-12). And while that passage is not *about* the Sabbath, it does underscore the connection between work and glorifying God.

So the Sabbath is not about inactivity but is about a different kind of activity than we do during the rest of the week. The activity prohibited was that which produces material prosperity, acquiring legitimate things we need to live but which can quickly and easily become idols. But nothing about the command to Sabbath rest prohibits the labor of love. Scripture says you should rest from "your work," but it never says you should rest from *God's* work.

This is the reinterpretation of God's Word that Jesus presents to the Pharisees. Then, he models its application. Rest is not the absence of all activity. Rest is the pursuit of doing what is good to do. The labor that *never* rests is the labor of goodness and mercy. This pleases God as it imitates God. This is what Jesus was doing in the synagogue before the eyes of the Pharisees, illuminating his role as lord of the Sabbath. Jesus has the authority to interpret the law correctly, and he has the ability to use even that law as a way to give his people rest. Scripture properly interpreted does just that – it helps us understand and therefore rest in God.

Rest is a Person

Rest as a theological category is found throughout
Scripture. Resting fully in God is precisely what was lost
in the Garden of Eden, so the gradual recovery of the state
of perfect biblical rest, culminating in the return of Jesus
and the institution of the new heavens and new earth, is
central to everything God is doing today, and everything
he has done since the Fall. All of God's work through all
time points to Jesus as the full interpretation of God.

Rightly interpreted, all Scripture leads to Jesus.
Every page of the Bible points to him. He is the Messiah
promised even before Adam and Eve were banished from
the Garden. He is the Savior who lived a sinless life and
hung on the cross to pay the price for our sins. And he is
the Lord who will return at the end. The rest in God that
was lost in Genesis 3 is being returned to us and will ultimately be fully returned to us in and through the person
and work of Jesus.

Had the Pharisees been paying attention, they might
have begun to realize this even before the whole matter
of eating from the grainfields and healing on the Sabbath.
For just before those encounters, Jesus made it plain, right
out in public:

> Come to me, all who labor and are heavy laden, and I
> will give you rest. Take my yoke upon you, and learn
> from me, for I am gentle and lowly in heart, and you
> will find rest for your souls. For my yoke is easy, and
> my burden is light. (Matthew 11:28-30)

Jesus is saying that if we learn from him and do the work that he does ("take my yoke upon you"), we will know rest. Rest is not produced by inactivity. It is produced by work – the right kind of work, the work that imitates the one who himself is our Rest. To rest is to take on the yoke of grace instead of the yoke of the Law (the yoke of the Pharisees). The way of rest is the way of imitation as we seek to be like him who always perfectly trusted his Father for everything.

In Matthew 11:29, Jesus cites Jeremiah 6:16, "Thus says the LORD: 'Stand by the roads, and look, and ask for the ancient paths, where the good way is; and walk in it, and find rest for your souls.'" Rest is walking on the paths that are good ways. Rest for our souls does not come from the absence of activity but the presence of doing good. Being merciful, even on the Sabbath, is imitating Jesus.

This is why in the New Testament we aren't just called to rest *on a day*. We are called to rest *in a person*. We rest in the good of the gospel. We rest in Jesus. The Sabbath is not about having a day of bed rest from everything. We walk and rest in the good of Christ's sacrifice. We do so knowing that even when we fail, he is gentle and humble.

Grace and the forgiveness of sin are the yoke of Jesus. And when Christians rest, we are to obey the command given by God to remember our salvation from the slavery of sin. Our Egypt is not a literal country from which we were rescued. Our Egypt is an all-pervasive slavery to sin. We are to reflect on this when we rest in God. This is what the Sabbath is about. We are no longer called to rest on a day. We are called to rest in a person.

I'm not taking sides on the question of how, exactly, Christians should observe a Sabbath day. But I am saying that to practice rest as God intends us to, whether on the Sabbath or at any other time, is to reflect on God's goodness in both creation and salvation. The command to rest was given corporately to the nation of Israel, and I believe it should be a corporate practice for the church.

For many of us, this is what Sunday meetings accomplish. We gather corporately as local bodies of believers to sing, celebrate, reflect, and express love and mercy to one another in word and deed. In all these things, we imitate and obey our triune God. In Matthew 12, Jesus interpreted the Sabbath rightly after the Pharisees had gotten it wrong for so long. He could interpret the Word correctly because he is the object of God's Word. He truly is lord of the Sabbath. It is all about him, so he is constantly explaining what the Scriptures mean and his interpretation is always right.

This is important for us to see. In Matthew 12, Jesus does more than correct the Pharisees. He does more than interpret Scripture rightly. He lays down a foundation for right interpretation. As we will see in the next chapter, there are breadcrumbs here for us to follow. And those breadcrumbs are not falling out of college-level textbooks. We find them by looking closely at how Jesus interprets Scripture. It really is that simple. No intelligence required. Well, maybe a little.

But God uses the foolish to shame the wise. Dummies can make a difference. If you have ever been overwhelmed by the very sharp thinkers that you know, if you have ever felt like you should be in a *Dumb and Dumber* sequel, then in the immortal words of Michael Jackson, "You are not alone. I am here with you."

So are a gazillion other believers. The question is, what now?

Five
FROM ME-OLOGY TO THEOLOGY

Recognizing the Obstacles to Interpretation

For the typical Christian, the skill of interpreting the Bible *the way Jesus did* has nearly become a lost art. When any group of believers relies too much on a relatively small group of Official Interpreters, bad things can happen.

Sometimes, interpreters are vitally necessary. We can be grateful that leaders rose up against a series of interpretive heresies in the early church, and that Martin Luther's aggressive campaign for a right interpretation of Scripture largely kicked off the Reformation. But where Christians have free access to the Bible (they didn't in Luther's day, nor do they in many places in the world today), an over-reliance on receiving from an elite group of interpreters can quickly take on a downside.

Let me put it this way: it is entirely biblical to learn from others, but it is altogether unbiblical to learn only from others. God's people should never neglect the fundamental *personal* responsibility of understanding his Word.

Every believer will stand before God and give an account for what they interpreted and applied. God will start with what each of us *knew Scripture to be saying*, not what we *thought* we understood second-hand from others. It is vitally important for all Christians to be imitators of Jesus in interpreting his Word.

Most everywhere American Christians go, we encounter Bible teachers. Not just in church. They are on TV, on the radio, and on podcasts. They tweet and blog and some of them even record rap albums. They wait for our attention in thousands of books and piles of magazines. And whether in print or video or audio, they can come to us on the screens of every digital device anyone can imagine.

I have no doubt that wherever the gospel is being accurately taught and the Bible accurately explained, this is a good thing. Paul celebrated the preaching of the gospel even when it was done from sinful motives (Philippians 1:12-15). But there is a downside, too. Just because it's the Bible being taught doesn't mean the fallen nature of creation isn't in play, mixing some significant bad in with the good. We naturally see every one of those teachers as a specialist, someone with a rare ability. They are not like us – so how can we possibly do what they do?

Surrounded by teachers and preachers and speakers and writers who are smarter and better educated and wiser than we are, it's easy to imagine that the path to understanding Scripture is only for the brave and brainy, the courageous Indiana Jones-type believer ready to travel the dark and dangerous caves of Hebrew and Koine

Greek. Most of us wouldn't even consider going that route. We can all too easily conclude that it is somebody else's job to be about the business of interpreting Scripture. Not our role, but theirs.

But that's not really true is it? *Have you not read?* is as much for us as it was for those who heard it from the lips of Jesus. There is a responsibility that comes with salvation.

God's self-revelation is in the book that we call the Bible. He has matched the content of that book to our capacity to understand, and he has given us the Spirit as Helper. Because of this, we can all use that book to grow in our relationship with God. We are called to interpret Scripture *alongside* our beloved theologians – not always behind them. Yes, they know more than we do, and we will often walk behind them in terms of sheer knowledge, but as Christians we must also be Bereans, who "received the word with all eagerness, examining the Scriptures daily to see if these things were so" (Acts 17:11). They didn't just say, " Well, Paul is smart and we're dummies so whatever he says goes." No! Those folks checked the Scriptures so that they could see if what he said was true.

Good teaching is a gift of God to his people. *But if that is how you are getting most of your Bible insight, something is seriously wrong.*

So how should we think of ourselves? Should we remain in relative biblical illiteracy our entire lives? If Jesus didn't teach that we need to go to school to under-stand the Scriptures, then how can we grow in biblical understanding?

Handling Scripture Like Jesus

One of the more interesting facts about the disciples is how uneducated they were. Those dudes were not the sharpest tools in the box, yet they changed the world. They did it by explaining God's Word to people and watching it take effect. I know I'm being simplistic here, but simple is the point. All believers should be able to interpret the Bible with little to no education in theological studies. Jesus showed us how to do that accurately. He laid out a simple interpretive grid that, if followed, can raise the level of understanding for anyone.

What is this interpretive grid that he has left us to imitate?

> That very day two of them were going to a village named Emmaus, about seven miles from Jerusalem, and they were talking with each other about all these things that had happened. While they were talking and discussing together, Jesus himself drew near and went with them. But their eyes were kept from recognizing him. And he said to them, "What is this conversation that you are holding with each other as you walk?" And they stood still, looking sad. Then one of them, named Cleopas, answered him, "Are you the only visitor to Jerusalem who does not know the things that have happened there in these days?" And he said to them, "What things?" And they said to him, "Concerning Jesus of Nazareth, a man who was a prophet mighty in deed and word before God and all the people, and how our chief priests and

> rulers delivered him up to be condemned to death,
> and crucified him. But we had hoped that he was
> the one to redeem Israel. Yes, and besides all this, it
> is now the third day since these things happened.
> Moreover, some women of our company amazed
> us. They were at the tomb early in the morning, and
> when they did not find his body, they came back
> saying that they had even seen a vision of angels, who
> said that he was alive. Some of those who were with
> us went to the tomb and found it just as the women
> had said, but him they did not see." And he said to
> them, "O foolish ones, and slow of heart to believe all
> that the prophets have spoken! Was it not necessary
> that the Christ should suffer these things and enter
> into his glory?" **And beginning with Moses and
> all the Prophets, he interpreted to them in all the
> Scriptures the things concerning himself.** (Luke
> 24:13-27)

Jesus interpreted the Scriptures, demonstrating that
they are about him, here and elsewhere. The process
of revealing how Scripture is about the Son was key to
the entire earthly life of Jesus. His life and his teaching
demonstrated that the Scriptures are all about him. And
with the help of the Holy Spirit – the same Holy Spirit
who helps us today – his disciples then went about the
business of imitating Jesus and explaining to others that
the Scriptures are all about him. It changed the world. It is
still changing the world.

The Bible is a big neon arrow pointing directly at

Jesus. All believers should read the Bible knowing that Jesus is the fulfillment of Old Testament prophecies and the guarantor of New Testament promises. Each page of Scripture is about Jesus.

* The Bible is not really *about* Abraham or David or any other merely human character.
* It's not about Israel or the church.
* It's not about Reformed or Arminian theology.
* It's not about dispensationalism or covenant theology.

These things are not irrelevant to Christianity. These and lots of other secondary matters can all contribute to our understanding of Scripture and the Christian life. But every one of these issues takes a back seat to the Savior. Everything in the Bible that *isn't* Jesus serves as a link in a chain that leads *to* Jesus. The whole thing, every page, is about Jesus. That doesn't make these other issues unimportant, just less important.

One more time, just to be clear.

* The Bible is not *about* archaeological findings.
* Or who wrote the various books.
* Or whether homosexuality or hospitality is the point of the Sodom and Gomorrah story.
* Or whether hell is a real, literal, permanent destination.

Do these questions matter? Sure they do. All of these are important issues. It's a good thing to be able to defend against arguments that dismiss or misrepresent God's

Word. But at some point, we as the church must bring the conversation back to what the Bible is *about*. It's about Jesus. If people aren't seeing that, it's because we often don't point it out. It is our responsibility to learn how to interpret the Scriptures the way Jesus did, not to get distracted by a thousand other things. And we can do that.

We can do it because in Luke 24 Jesus gives a hermeneutics course like no other. That simply means he tells us how to interpret Scripture. He shows us how we can learn to interpret our Bibles without any formal training.

This does take some time and effort, but it's worth it. More importantly, God expects us to do this.

Handling Scripture Like the Disciples

The church is called to evangelism and discipleship. Each of these involves accurate interpretation and accurate application.

Evangelism. Look closely in the book of Acts. Whether from Peter (Acts 2 and 3), Stephen (Acts 7), Philip (Acts 8), or Paul (Acts 13), each gospel presentation *interprets* the Scriptures as being about Jesus, and it is typically followed by an encouragement to *apply* the Scriptures by repenting.

Discipleship. The epistles teach and exhort us to apply Scripture so that we live for the glory of God. They do this by interpretation and application, with *every* teaching and **every** exhortation ultimately grounded in the gospel, which is grounded in the person and work of Jesus.

Should we not learn from these examples? Why should interpreting the Bible be different for us today? Our calling is the same as that of the early disciples: to imitate Jesus through evangelism and discipleship. And we do that by interpreting the Scriptures rightly and then applying them. Jesus, the primary object of Scripture and the primary interpreter of Scripture, has given us this interpretive example to follow.

My concern, though, is that when Christians want to understand what the Bible teaches, we often go first to *something other than the Bible*. We go to books instead of The Book. We hop online to find out what our favorite preacher has to say about a certain passage or subject.

Sometimes I wonder: how did people interpret and apply their Bibles before there were commentaries? How did those early church fathers know what to say and do? The simple answer is that they read their Bibles, meditated on their Bibles, prayed over their Bibles, and applied their Bibles. Over time, knowledge becomes wisdom. With great patience and careful instruction, information does indeed become application.

As we read and study our Bibles, we should consistently ask the question, "How does this section of Scripture point to Jesus?" You will not always see a direct connection, and you don't want to force it so that you lose sight of the author's original intent. But we must learn how to read our Bibles contextually and Christologically: read each passage in light of what was happening when the author wrote it, and in light of who Christ is since he has fulfilled *all Scripture*. Believers can and should read our Bibles with full confidence that all Scripture is about Jesus.

In various places, in various ways, and from the perspective of different points in history, the Bible tells us who Jesus is, what he will do, what he has done, and what he is doing:

- Sometimes the Scriptures are preparing us for Jesus' coming (like Exodus, Leviticus, Isaiah, and Jeremiah).
- Sometimes they show us that he's here (see Matthew, Mark, Luke, and John).
- Sometimes they explain the significance of who he is and what he did (like Ephesians and Hebrews).
- Sometimes they show us how to live because of him (like James, 1 Peter, and 1 John).
- And sometimes the Scriptures tell us he's coming back (like 1 Thessalonians and Revelation).

Our responsibility as believers is to interpret Scripture accurately. That's also one of the primary ways we imitate God. If you start and stay with the idea that the Bible is about Jesus, you really can't go wrong.

But if you drift from that idea, you will go seriously wrong.

Me-ology and the Obstacles to Interpretation

As we read the Bible, we should ask ourselves what the passage before us is saying about Jesus or how it points to Jesus. Sounds simple enough, right? Unfortunately, it isn't. Two primary obstacles – false expectations and sin – stand in the way of our ability to do this consistently. Although these two are closely related and often interwoven, they are still worth discussing separately. Together or on their own, these can have a huge negative impact on our interpretation and application of God's Word. To put it another way, our me-ology gets in the way of our theology.

Me-ology, Part 1: Selfish Expectations

The Pharisees hated Jesus. They hated him consistently, predictably, and passionately. They hated him for embarrassing them. They hated him for re-interpreting their oppressive rules. They hated him for showing others how to interpret Scripture accurately. They hated him for the way he interpreted Scripture and applied it to them.

Jesus interpreted in word and deed. His explanation often led to illustration, which led to Pharisaical frustration. The Pharisees just never came out looking too good when they tussled with Jesus. They were hatin'!

It's the same with us, if we're honest. When Jesus interprets his Word to us, we can hate it too.

Like the Pharisees, we are prone to think that our interpretation of God's Word is *the* interpretation of God's Word. We read a passage, think about it, come up with an interpretation, make application from that interpretation, and move on. In many cases this is a good way to interact with our Bibles, especially with regard to imperatives – passages that tell us what to do or not to do. But this doesn't work nearly as well when we get to some of Scripture's promises. In fact, this is the area in which we imitate the Pharisees most closely. We read one of the many wonderful promises in the Bible, (mis)interpret it in a way that we find desirable, and expect God to act according to our me-ological interpretation. We make the promises mean what we want them to mean, and we then imagine God will back us up by allowing events to go the way we think they should.

Take for example one of the most beloved verses in all of Scripture (at least in my circles), and one that I have regularly used and misused myself. Romans 8:28 says, "And we know that for those who love God all things work together for good, for those who are called according to his purpose." This verse has become for many people the blank check of God's sovereignty guaranteeing that everything will be easy. When difficulty comes, we are quick to remind one another, "God is sovereign," and he absolutely is. So we utter the phrase and point to Romans 8:28, but how often are we left with the impression – and how often do we try to *give* the impression – that this means everything will turn out according to our preferences?

I have heard Romans 8:28 used to counsel people that their child will repent and believe the gospel. That could happen, but the verse doesn't promise that.

I have heard Romans 8:28 used to offer comfort that someone will be healed or get married or be offered the job they want. Again, those things may happen. But there is nothing anywhere in the Bible, and certainly nothing in Romans 8:28, to guarantee it!

With Romans 8:28 or some other promise as our (misinterpreted) bedrock, we can act just like the Pharisees. We expect God to line up with our interpretations and "work this out for our good." Of course, our "good" is often not the same as God's. What we think will happen in many cases does not. Why? It's actually because God is sovereign.

God does not reveal to us the specifics of his will for our individual lives. The Bible gives us a very clear picture of God's larger plan and purpose in and through the gospel, but the specific part each of us plays in that plan remains pretty much a mystery. Yet somehow we often place our hope in the details of our interpretation rather than in the goodness and mercy of our sovereign and loving God. Once this happens, we eagerly wait for God to make good on his "promise" to us – when, in fact, it's nothing more than our preference.

There is a difference between what we pray and what God has promised. Prayer is often about what we want God to give us. But promises are what God tells us he has already given us in Christ. All of those promises *will* be ours, but many will not be experienced in this life. That is why we have hope for the next life.

It is easy for us to place our hope in what we think sovereignty *means in a particular circumstance* rather than in the simple fact that God is sovereign, faithful, and good. When we insist on seeing God's promises fulfilled in this life, according to our me-ological timetable and desired outcomes, we can quickly grow indignant at God for not coming through. We grow angry, bitter, and confused.

We withdraw from God. We come to think of him as unloving, and we imagine we would do a much better job in his position.

After a while, what he *has* done for us disappears from view, and all we can see anymore is what he hasn't done. We refuse to give him glory for who he is and what he has done, and we judge him on false criteria that we have fabricated out of our own sinfulness and limitations. We become Pharisees. The only things missing are the tasseled robes.

What we are trying to do is restrict God to our interpretation of his Word. He should do what we prefer him to do. He should be what we prefer him to be. That would make him a good God. That would prove he is, in fact, sovereign. But God is not required to submit to our interpretation of his Word. In not acting according to what we think he should do, God mercifully reminds us that he, not our interpretations, is sovereign.

God acts according to who he is, not what we want him to be. When our expectations are not met, we must believe that whatever God allows to happen is the right interpretation of his Word as applied to the situation. Scripture certainly is about what God promises to do for us in Jesus, but even more than that, Scripture is about Jesus himself. It's about who he is before it's about what he does. Our lack of faith in God comes from faulty interpretation of the Scriptures.

For example, if we want to interpret Romans 8:28 correctly, we must allow Romans 8:29 to help us. "For those whom he foreknew he also predestined to be conformed to the image of his Son, in order that he might be the firstborn among many brothers." The "good" that God works out for us is *being made like Jesus.*

We are becoming more like Jesus through the circumstances that God allows to happen, even (maybe especially) when they don't fit our preferences. This involves change. Do you really think you would change into the image of his Son if everything in your life went smoothly? Wouldn't you just stay exactly as you are right now? Why risk messing up a good thing by changing? No, more often than not, change comes through suffering, not from the status quo. We usually must be forced into the kind of change we most need – the kind of change that most glorifies God. Reading Romans 8:28, our expectations should lean *toward* suffering, not toward being rescued from suffering. Despite what you will hear from some teachers who manage to get a lot of airtime, perpetual blessing is not the Christian life – at least not our definition of perpetual blessing. God is sovereign in making us like his Son. That is the way of change, the way of increasing Christ-likeness.

Bad interpretation reads selfish expectations into Scripture, but good interpretation expects Scripture to describe and produce Christ-centered change, even at great cost to those selfish expectations I've still got rolling around in me. This is the way of true blessing.

Me-ology, Part 2: Selective Attention
The other way bad interpretation happens is when we choose to read the Bible selectively. We read only what

we believe is immediately relevant to us. Sin tries to convince us that the Bible is about us, and therefore we need not concern ourselves with the parts of the Bible that we can't relate to. *If you can't apply it, deny it.* This kind of thinking prevents us from being able to understand God's Word as we should. But this is another form of *me*-ology, not theology. When I decide that some parts of the Bible are beneficial to me and others are not, I have reached a dangerous cliff. Below are sharp rocks, a low tide, and imminent spiritual death should I jump. Most of us are smart enough not to jump, but we're plenty dumb enough to try to climb down. That is, we don't deny the faith by jumping off, but we creep downward in self-centered interpretation of Scripture, and before we realize it, we're so far away from God.

For many years I did just that. I read the Bible very selfishly, staying away from some of the best parts because they didn't "immediately benefit me." I was a true me-ologian. My limited reading of the Bible gave me a limited God. I read small and believed smaller. There were times I would argue that the God in the Old Testament was angry and that the God of the New Testament was nice. I had no understanding of how all the parts of the Bible connected.

I led groups and used small portions of the Bible to try and help people comprehend a big God – a God that I wasn't even seeing. My Bible reading was lazy, but most of the time it was just selfish. I read the Bible for personal benefit only. Had I read certain parts of the Old Testament sooner, I might have learned from men like Saul.

In 1 Samuel 15, the sad tale of Israel's first king whom

we looked at earlier in this book, we find another example of how not to interpret God's Word.

> And Samuel said to Saul, "The Lord sent me to anoint you king over his people Israel; now therefore listen to the words of the Lord. Thus says the Lord of hosts, 'I have noted what Amalek did to Israel in opposing them on the way when they came up out of Egypt. Now go and strike Amalek and devote to destruction all that they have. Do not spare them, but kill both man and woman, child and infant, ox and sheep, camel and donkey.'" (1 Samuel 15:1-3)

God gave Saul a clear charge through Samuel, and it seemed relatively simple, if potentially strange to our modern ears (but that's a different topic for a different day): destroy Amalek, all the people and all the animals.

Saul, a military guy who knows how to take and give orders, gathers an army 200,000 strong and goes to war with the Amalekites. Here is Scripture's record of what happened:

> And Saul defeated the Amalekites from Havilah as far as Shur, which is east of Egypt. And he took Agag the king of the Amalekites alive and devoted to destruction all the people with the edge of the sword. But Saul and the people spared Agag and the best of the sheep and of the oxen and of the fattened calves and the lambs, and all that was good, and would not utterly destroy them. All that was despised and

worthless they devoted to destruction. (1 Samuel 15.7-11)

The two words most obviously out of place in this passage are *alive* and *spared*. What in the world happened here? How did Saul go from "Do not spare them" to "would not utterly destroy them"? He did the opposite of what he was commanded!

We know the reason for this is sin, but let's look closely at the manner in which sin was working. After Saul leaves the battle site, Samuel the prophet goes to meet him, and Saul immediately says, "I have performed the commandment of the LORD" (1 Samuel 15:13). But God had already told Samuel that Saul had disobeyed. Besides, Samuel can hear just fine. So he says to Saul, "What then is this bleating of the sheep in my ears and the lowing of the oxen that I hear?" (1 Samuel 15:14).

Even then, Saul tells a partial truth: "They have brought them from the Amalekites, for the people spared the best of the sheep and of the oxen to sacrifice to the Lord your God, and the rest we have devoted to destruction." God had clearly "devoted to destruction" every man and animal of the Amalekites, and Saul's job was to move everything from the Devoted column to the Destruction column. Everything. But here in Samuel's ears was ample proof that Saul had ignored God's order. To understand how serious this is, we need to see what "devoted to destruction" meant to God:

But no devoted thing that a man devotes to the Lord,

of anything that he has, whether man or beast, or of his inherited field, shall be sold or redeemed; every devoted thing is most holy to the Lord. No one devoted, who is to be devoted for destruction from mankind, shall be ransomed; he shall surely be put to death. (Leviticus 27:28-29)

From God's perspective, nothing devoted to destruction can be ransomed. It cannot be spared. Its destination is doom, and God says it shall surely be put to death.

What Saul did was far more serious than even he realized. This was direct disobedience to God and his Law. As Samuel confronted Saul, the underlying sins became clear. Saul wanted to suggest that his main sin was fear of man: "I have sinned, for I have transgressed the commandment of the Lord and your words, because I feared the people and obeyed their voice" (1 Samuel 15:24). But it was clear to Samuel (see verse 23) that Saul was also guilty of presumption, rebellion, and idolatry.

The big tent in which Saul's sins were congregating was his self-worship. In the face of an unambiguous command, Saul trusted and obeyed himself above God. He gave selective attention to God's clear commands. Saul's view of God's Word was selfish, a matter of me-ology instead of theology, so his interpretation of God's Word turned obedience into convenience. God's command became optional. It went from **must** do to *might do*.

Me-ological reinterpretation is one of the main ways sin affects our interpretation and application of God's

Word. We can think, "What does this passage do for me," more than "What does this say about God?" Sin says, "Reading the Bible is really all about how I can grow as a person, so I will focus on the parts seem to help me the most." Sin says, "Stick to the Proverbs and Psalms that really speak to you. Stick to the Gospels and letters with commands that tell you how to live." Sin says, "Read only what you can apply," so we get lazy and complain about the parts of Scripture we can't relate to. If the Bible doesn't appeal to us, we are not excited about reading it, but we figure that's just fine.

This limits our ability to know who God is because our view of God will be directly connected to what we read and apply from his Word. If our Bible reading is limited, our ability to interpret our Bible will be limited as well. This is how Scripture gets taken out of context. Scripture interprets Scripture: you must read one part to understand another part. So if we don't read the Scriptures we won't interpret God's Word rightly, and if we don't interpret God's Word rightly then our application may not be right either. When our interpretation and application are wrong, our view of God will be wrong too.

At that point, reading God's Word becomes all about personal impact rather than personal relationship. We start believing the Bible is about a God who meets our needs instead of a God who lets us meet his Son. Sin places self above God, so it makes sense that sin will tempt us to look for ourselves in God's Word, skipping the parts that seem irrelevant. How long has it been since you've read Leviticus, Second Chronicles, Zephaniah, or Malachi?

Why not read these? These books teach us amazing things about Jesus. If we examine ourselves, we may find that those books don't appeal to us because we don't think they're beneficial for us. We need to stop being self-focused when we approach God's Word.

What Now? Application

The truth is that on most of the pages of the Bible, you and I don't appear at all. But God is in every syllable. Let's read the entirety of Scripture because we truly believe that all of it is God-breathed. Every part of this book reveals to us the nature, character, and actions of the God we worship, so we must not see any part as unhelpful or irrelevant. We must not limit the Bible to something that is simply "good for us." It is infinitely more than that. It is the very Word of God.

One way we can fight the temptation to view the Bible selfishly is to commit to reading and understanding every book in the Bible. It takes time. It takes effort. It takes the Holy Spirit. But it will change your view of God and his Word.

Let's learn to read genealogies and the locations where the tribes settled into the Promised Land. Let's read the obscure and difficult prophecies that can seem as irrelevant as the names of distant galaxies. Let's not just read what we think will "help us." Let's read what God has *given us*, knowing and trusting and believing that every page is a good and perfect gift. If we do this, it will affect both our interpretation and our application of God's Word. Because Jesus the Word of God has given us his Spirit, we really do have what we need to interpret God's Word rightly. We can and should have confidence that the broad and deep reading of Scripture will fuel our capacity to rightly interpret God's Word so that we might rightly apply God's Word. And when we fail – which we will – the broad and deep reading of Scripture will help us remember that Jesus gave his life for the times when we fail him.

Jesus is *the* Interpreter, and every Christian is *an* interpreter. Imitation over education.

Again, education isn't bad. I encourage you to pursue it if you can. It will make a huge difference in helping you to interpret Scripture. I'm not calling for picket lines in front the local Bible college. If you feel called to that kind of education, go! But if you can't go, may you grow to read, interpret, and apply God's Word rightly, for if you are a Christian there is nothing standing in your way.

As you read, remember first and foremost that Jesus is the primary interpreter of God's Word. Then follow Jesus' example by reading the Bible clearly in the knowledge that it's all about him. He's the object of Scripture.

We can do this. In fact, we must do this if we are to be good disciples of Jesus. It will be hard, but it is not impossible. God has given us his Spirit to guide us into all truth. We know the framework of Scripture because we know the Object and Interpreter of Scripture.

Now, go with God!

Inductive Bible Studies for Women by Keri Folmar

JOY! – A Bible Study on Philippians for Women

bit.ly/JoyStudy

GRACE: A Bible Study on Ephesians for Women

bit.ly/GraceStudy

FAITH: A Bible Study on James for Women

bit.ly/FaithStudy

"It is hard to imagine a better inductive Bible Study tool."
–Diane Schreiner

Recently added to the series: a 2-volume study of Mark's Gospel, plus a study on Titus!

Keri's studies have been endorsed by...

Kathleen Nielson is author of the *Living Word Bible Studies;* Director of Women's Initiatives, The Gospel Coalition; and wife of Niel, who served as President of Covenant College from 2002 to 2012.

Diane Schreiner – wife of professor, author, and pastor Tom Schreiner, and mother of four grown children – has led women's Bible studies for more than 20 years.

Connie Dever is author of *The Praise Factory* children's ministry curriculum and wife of Pastor Mark Dever, President of 9 Marks Ministries.

Kristie Anyabwile, holds a history degree from NC State University, and is married to Thabiti, currently a church planter in Washington, D.C., and a Council Member for The Gospel Coalition.

Gloria Furman is a pastor's wife in the Middle East and author of *Glimpses of Grace* and *Treasuring Christ When Your Hands Are Full.*

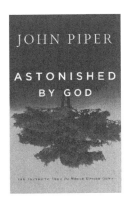

Astonished by God
Ten Truths to Turn the World Upside Down

John Piper | 192 pages

Turn your world on its head.

bit.ly/AstonishedbyGod

The Joy Project:
An Introduction to Calvinism
(with Study Guide)

Tony Reinke
Foreword by John Piper | 168 pages

True happiness isn't found. It finds you.

bit.ly/JOYPROJECT

"But God..."
The Two Words at the Heart of the Gospel

Casey Lute | 100 pages

Just two words…Understand their use in Scripture, and you will never be the same.

bit.ly/ButGOD

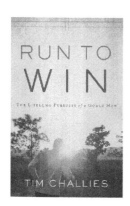

Run to Win:
The Lifelong Pursuits of a Godly Man

Tim Challies | 163 pages

Plan to run, train to run…run to win.

bit.ly/RUN2WIN

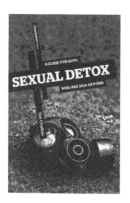

Sexual Detox
A Guide for Guys Who Are Sick of Porn

Tim Challies | 90 pages

Reorient your understanding of sex, according to God's plan for this great gift.

bit.ly/SEXUALDETOX

Torn to Heal
God's Good Purpose in Suffering

Mike Leake | 87 pages

"The most concise, readable, and helpful theology of suffering." (David Murray)

bit.ly/TORN2H

Advance!

Tim Challies | 55 pages

How can young adults make the best use of these years? Be like Jesus and advance!...in wisdom, stature, and favor with God and man.

bit.ly/Challies-Advance

The Character of the Christian

Tim Challies | 54 pages

Learn to be a model of Christian maturity.

bit.ly/Challies-Character

Set an Example

Tim Challies | 48 pages

Set an example. Be an example. Make your life a beautiful work of art.

bit.ly/Challies-Example

Who Am I?
Identity in Christ

Jerry Bridges | 91 pages

Jerry Bridges unpacks Scripture to give the Christian eight clear, simple, interlocking answers to one of the most essential questions of life.

bit.ly/WHOAMI

Getting Back in the Race
The Cure for Backsliding

Joel R. Beeke | 103 pages

Learn the diagnosis. experience the cure.

bit.ly/THERACE

Licensed to Kill
A Field Manual for Mortifying Sin

Brian G. Hedges | 101 pages

Your soul is a war zone—know your enemy and learn to fight

bit.ly/L2Kill